Not your average

50TH BIRTHDAY
PARTY
Guest Book

Welcome to my Birthday

Flip to any page and dive in. Doodle, draw and leave a comment!

Thank you!

Guest Self Portraits

Don't forget to sign your art!

Guest Self Portraits

HAPPY BIRTH DAY

I just wanted to say...

Bucket list suggestions

Bucket list suggestions

leaf

a message

you can doodle here!

Reasons

you're a star!

Share your advice

for the future

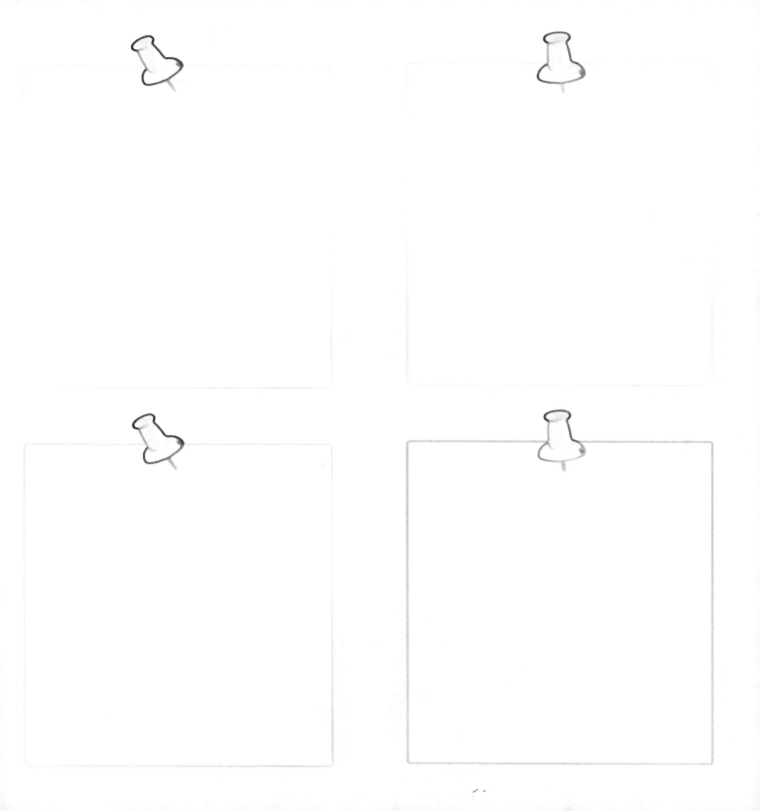

Thank you for

your memories

Birthday

Wishes

Birthday Wishes

Share a secret..

Guest creativity page

draw, write, doodle!

Happy Birthday

I just wanted to say...

Guest Artwork

Don't forget to sign your art!

Bucket list
suggestions

Bucket list
suggestions

leaf

a message

you can doodle here!

Reasons

you're a star!

Thank you for

your memories

Birthday

Wishes

Guest creativity page

draw, write, doodle!

Guest Self Portraits

I just wanted to say...

Share your advice

for the future

Birthday
Wishes

Sweet Thoughts

leaf

a message

Event Highlights

Event Highlights

Event menu:

Guest list:

_____

_____

_____

_____

_____

_____

_____

_____

_____

_____

_____

_____

_____

_____

_____

_____

_____

_____

_____

_____

_____

_____

_____

_____

Guest list:

_____   _____

_____   _____

_____   _____

_____   _____

_____   _____

_____   _____

_____   _____

_____   _____

_____   _____

_____   _____

_____   _____

_____   _____

Guest list:

_____
_____
_____
_____
_____
_____
_____
_____
_____
_____
_____
_____
_____

_____
_____
_____
_____
_____
_____
_____
_____
_____
_____
_____
_____
_____

Guest list:

_____   _____

_____   _____

_____   _____

_____   _____

_____   _____

_____   _____

_____   _____

_____   _____

_____   _____

_____   _____

_____   _____

_____   _____

Guest list:

_____

_____

_____

_____

_____

_____

_____

_____

_____

_____

_____

_____

_____

_____

_____

_____

_____

_____

_____

_____

_____

_____

Guest list:

_____   _____

_____   _____

_____   _____

_____   _____

_____   _____

_____   _____

_____   _____

_____   _____

_____   _____

_____   _____

_____   _____

_____   _____

Add your photos here!

Add your photos here!

Add your photos here!

Add your
photos here!

Add your
photos here!

Add your
photos
here!

Add your photos here!

Add your
photos here!

Add your photos here!

Gift Log

Guest	Gift	Thanks

Gift Log

Guest	Gift	Thanks

Gift Log

Guest	Gift	Thanks

Gift Log

Guest	Gift	Thanks

Gift Log

Guest	Gift	Thanks

Gift Log

Guest	Gift	Thanks

Made in the USA
Monee, IL
16 January 2023

25383655R00070